Investing

Investing Secrets Revealed That Will Enable You To Amass Your Own Fortune

(How To Identify Undervalued Stocks To Outperform The Market)

Maynard Estrada

TABLE OF CONTENT

Shares/Stocks/Equities 1

Deferred Satisfaction 17

Stop Handling Your Own Mess! 34

The Future Requires A Benchmark Standard . 57

Earnest Money Deposit Not Refundable 86

Two Lost Transactionscaper 98

Investors With A High Net Worth Versus Small Investors 107

Three Genuine Currencies 117

Shares/Stocks/Equities 128

Developing My Company And My Life 143

Shares/Stocks/Equities

Although they are comparative terms, there are distinctions between them.

The term stocks is more inclusive. It represents a share of ownership. Typically, shares represent a portion of responsibility for a particular company.

Stocks are divided into shares; the smallest division of a company's stock is a share. Every share of stock represents an offer to invest in a company. For instance, if a person claims 1% of a company's stock, you can say they have 1% of the company's offer.

Equity represents ownership of an organization's assets minus its liabilities.

Stocks are small units issued by a company that can be bought and traded.

Why do companies provide them? It allows them to raise funds and locate investors.

When you acquire an offer, you acquire a stake in a company and become a shareholder.

You may have a few privileges and benefits as an investor. You could, for instance, deliberate on business matters or receive profit payments.

The dividend payment is a portion of the advantages paid to investors by a company. A company is not required to generate profits. They can be paid on a recurring basis or as a one-time payment.

Shares do not provide a guarantee of profit, and there is risk associated with all investments. Costs may rise or fall.

You can purchase shares on your own or merge your funds with others in a joint venture. This is referred to as a fund.

How long would it be prudent for you to make contributions? Preferably, a considerable amount of time to allow for the passage of time in case you incur a loss due to market fluctuations.

If you can't hold off your cash for that long and require access to it sooner, then offers are probably not the best option for you at this time.

According to the idiom, do not lock up your assets in one location. It is too risky to hold stock in a single company, and if the value of an investment falls, you will lose money.

What are the advantages of stocks?

- You could potentially receive dividends
- They can cover costs • Adaptable

What are the disadvantages of stocks?

- You probably won't get dividends • Risky

- Market cost can fluctuate

As a first-time investor, a safe option for you would be to invest in a stocks&shares Isas. An Isa is a single bank account with securities and dividends. Isas allow you to invest in a variety of investments and funds.

An Isa is the British equivalent of the American IRA.

You can grow your money in two ways with an offer: if the price of the offer increases, you can generate a profit (it will be worth more than when you purchased it), and if the company decides to pay you dividends.

The easiest method to acquire shares is through an online offer management platform. You are able to purchase shares from any company listed on the stock exchange.

You ought to establish a trading account. After opening and funding your account, you are able to purchase equities through the dealer's website.

Other alternatives include using a full-service stockbroker or purchasing shares directly from the company.

How would you select stocks? An excellent place to start is by researching companies you have interacted with as a customer.

What quantity of deals would you be wise to acquire? The overwhelming majority may anticipate holding between ten and twenty stocks.

If you wish to purchase from the London Stock Exchange or the New York Stock Exchange, an intermediary is required. Additionally, they will charge you a fee and frequently work on commission.

What does an offer cost? It fluctuates in response to market demand from buyers and sellers. If demand is significant, costs will also increase.

There are several fees you should be aware of:

• Account fees. This may be delayed depending on the number of trades you conduct.

• Inactivity fees. This could be assessed if your account exceeds the predetermined minimum number of transactions. Because they want you to remain with them, relatively few businesses impose this fee at present.

• Buying or selling. Each time you exchange shares, a fee is assessed.

• Stamp taxation. When purchasing shares, you typically pay a 0.5% transaction fee to the exchange. The only party responsible for payment is the purchaser.

Dividend Investing

This is a method for purchasing dividend-paying securities in order to profit from your investments.

Dividends are payments made by a partnership to its investors. When you own securities that generate profits, you receive a portion of the organization's earnings.

If the company you own stock in has a profit reinvestment plan, you can choose to have your profits reinvested to purchase additional shares rather than receiving them as a dividend.

Regular profit pay is a reliable and secure method of building a nest fund.

Companies that pay out 60% or less of their income as profits are generally safer investments because they are predictable.

Consider organizations that have a history of stable pay and cash flow.

The majority of pay from profits is taxed as common pay, but qualified profit equities held for a longer period (at least 60 days) are taxed at the lower capital increases charge rates.

Bonds

This is the juncture at which a credit is made to an organization or the government. They will provide securities when they need to raise funds to support initiatives.

The primary distinction between a security and a credit is that a security can be traded. There is usually a market where they can be traded. Credits are typically non-transferable arrangements between institutions and customers.

Bonds charge loan fees. The loan fees may be variable or fixed. A security has an expiration date, and when that date arrives, you should receive your money in full.

What is the bond's cost? • The creditworthiness of the person or entity providing the security. The bond is more hazardous the lower its rating. Continuously evaluate the guarantor's track record to determine if they are dependable or hazardous.

• The time remaining until maturity • The interest rate

You can present the attachment to various financial supporters. You are not required to remain with it until its expiration date.

What benefits do bonds offer?

- You are compensated with revenue payments • You receive all the money you contributed if you remain until the end • You can sell it for a profit

What are the downsides?

- Companies can default on their payments to you • If the financing cost decreases, so does the amount of your return

You may observe a security with a higher loan fee, but this indicates that the default risk is higher the higher the financing cost.

Avoid contributing solely based on the advertised financing cost. If the loan fee is high, it indicates the securities are riskier, and you have a greater chance of losing your entire investment.

When financing costs increase, bond prices decline, and vice versa. The loan cost hazard occurs when anticipated interest rates fluctuate. In the event that the loan rate rises, you will be left with a security returning below market rates.

The greater the potential for development, the greater the possibility that interest rates will increase.

There are two methods for generating income by investing in bonds.

The first option is to retain these securities until their maturity date and collect revenue installments. Typically, security premiums are paid twice per year.

The subsequent step is to sell them for a higher price than you initially paid.

You can also invest in security reserves, which are formed when a group of investors combine their funds so that an asset manager can purchase a large number of individual bonds.

There are four fundamental categories of bonds:

- Commercial. They are granted by institutions. Unlike shares, bonds issued by organizations do not confer ownership rights. They are less secure securities, but they typically compensate with higher rates of interest.

- Government bonds. Given by the government agency. It is a method for legislators to raise money without raising taxes. They can be an excellent option for the portfolio's generally secure portion.

- Municipal securities. Presented by cities, states, and counties.

- Agency obligations. Presented by government-affiliated institutions

The market interest rate determines the day-to-day value of an obligation. When selecting bonds, maturity and duration should be considered. Bonds with extended maturities will be significantly more affected by changes in average loan costs. Due to fluctuations in loan costs, securities with extended maturities are subject to a greater degree of risk; consequently, they offer higher yields (respects) and are therefore more attractive to investors.

• Premium. A few organizations assign a FICO score to each security in order to evaluate its quality. The yield decreases as the borrower's FICO score increases.

You can lose money on a security if you sell it before the maturity date for less than what you paid for it, or if the guarantor defaults on payments.

Typically, the duration over which you receive revenue payments from securities is two years.

Due to the fact that they do not all pay at the same time, investing in multiple securities can result in more regular payments.

It is possible to construct a security portfolio yielding monthly income. This can be obtained by purchasing various securities (typically six) that pay a premium on other dates.

Bonds are less susceptible to monetary loss than equities. Therefore, acquiring a few securities and a few equities can reduce portfolio losses. Bonds can be obtained from a number of sources, including investment and commercial institutions, brokers, and corporations.

The minimum investment required to purchase a single security is approximately $1,000, but securities are typically sold in increments of $5,000.

Deferred Satisfaction

The majority of individuals require instant access to the finer items in life, such as expensive home furnishings, luxury automobiles, and boats. This is reasonable, but to become financially independent, you must exercise discretion. I am not recommending that you live frugally, but within your means.

There will be times when you must decide if you genuinely require a new vehicle, or if you can make minor repairs to your current vehicle and survive for a few years without one. Even though it may be difficult to make the decision to wait, you will ultimately be happier if you do.

Consider the utility. Do you require a car to get to work? Indeed, you do. Do you want to drive a $50,000 BMW to work, or would a $25,000 Ford suffice?

Do you need a television? A large number of persons would agree. Do you desire a $10,000 home theater, or would a $500 Sony suffice?

I presume you already know the answer.

A secondary consideration is that if you must endorse it, you cannot afford the price. This applies to everything except for your first vehicle and land purchase. When you take care of your vehicle, you should set aside two or three years' worth of payments for your next vehicle using the amount you were paying on your installment. If you purchase vehicles that are a few years old, you will save approximately 40% off the price of a new vehicle, despite the fact that only 10% of the vehicle's existence has been utilized. In my previous neighborhoods, many of my neighbors attempted to "one-up" one another by purchasing expensive SUVs. My spouse and I both drive late-model vehicles, but neither of us has an auto loan. Our automobiles are not the finest, but they are paid off. It is more satisfying to know that our vehicle is paid off than to operate a more expensive vehicle with a payment.

This hypothesis holds true for everything that degrades. What good is it to have the most exquisite television or sound system if you must make monthly payments and their value decreases each month?

I am able to discern your thoughts, which is more difficult than one might assume. You have worked hard for your money, and it is only right that you value it. In any event, the two years of contentment you will derive from your new extra-large flat-screen television until a more modern model becomes available are brief. Investing that sum in a rental property, however, will generate a steady income that will enable you to buy a new television every two years. Can your current television do that?

After completing my first land swap and receiving a credit for the enhancements, I may have spent the money on random items. It would have been incredible to acquire a more comfortable vehicle and go on a purchasing spree. However, Cindy and I realized that we had requested the credit because the properties were in a deplorable state and required urgent repairs and upgrades. Over the subsequent half-year, we invested every cent into the properties, and as a result, we were able to nearly double the rents on them. This allowed the properties to increase their positive income and contributed to their overall value. Following this, we renegotiated two or three of the properties and spent some cash. All things considered, we collectively earn money… to spend it! Nonetheless, practical wisdom must be utilized to ensure that you are still achieving your current and long-term objectives. After only half a year, we were able to acquire everything we required, and in the interim, we had developed substantial value in the properties.

We had the most intelligent remedy possible: properties that were profitable for us and a new television.

Debt-to-Income Ratio

The two greatest obstacles to overcome when purchasing a property for investment purposes are how to formulate the initial investment and how to generate sufficient income to support the new obligation. The final option is commonly known as the pay-to-obligation ratio.

Many institutions will allow you to use up to 44% of your income to pay off debts. This includes Mastercards, vehicle advances, your mortgage, and real estate speculation contracts. It is easy to see how having an additional car payment would increase your debt-to-income ratio and negatively impact your ability to obtain a loan.

You're probably pondering how, with your income and expenses, you could afford to purchase an investment property. You don't need to qualify all alone. The investment property will generate income, which can be used to offset the mortgage payment. In any event, banks will typically only accept 75% of the rent payment, after which they will deduct the guideline, premium, protection, and local fees. The difference will be the entire compensation (or misfortune) by which your income can be altered.

That may sound intriguing, but it's actually quite simple. Consider that you are purchasing a four-unit condominium for $200,000. The monthly payment and market rents are $550 per unit, totaling $2,200. To obtain your new month-to-month income, you must increase your total rental payment by 0.75, or 75%. Your bank-modified monthly pay is $1,650.

Now, we expect you to make a 10% initial investment and sign a 30-year contract. Under these conditions, your monthly consolidated rule and interest payment will be approximately $1,200. Add to this the monthly local fees of approximately $200 and protection fees of approximately $100. For bank approval purposes, your total expenses amount to $1,500. Subtract this amount from your $1,650 monthly income, and add this $150 to your salary to help you qualify for the loan. In Chapters 4 and 5,

I will demonstrate how to calculate your actual revenue and expenses, but for the time being, it is essential to understand what the bank considers to be income.

Don't Give Up Your Day Job...Yet

I am aware, as are the majority of people, that you are presumably quitting your regular employment. Everyone yearns for the day when they will be financially independent. Despite the fact that investing in land is unquestionably the quickest path to wealth, it is not a get-rich-quick scheme. Overall, there are numerous benefits for first-time financial supporters.

You can easily invest in land in your spare time, as it is not a particularly time-intensive endeavor. When you've selected and closed on a property, it's extremely simple to maintain, typically requiring two to three hours per month per property.

I would recommend that you self-manage your first few properties. This will necessitate an investment, but it is essential for two reasons. In the beginning, you will be cash-strapped; however, by paying yourself first, you can save money. Second, it will equip you with the tools necessary to manage a property. Thus, when your property superintendent informs you of a lie in the future, you will have the experience to recognize it.

Once you are prepared to hire a property manager, it is essential to observe the ideal candidate. If you hire the right property manager, you will quickly realize that it does not cost significantly more than managing the property yourself (unless you also perform maintenance). Depending on the age, size, and location of the property, the standard supervisory group charges between 5% and 10%. The supervisory group typically has a support individual on staff and will charge you less to repair a particular issue than if you hired a project worker.

Additionally, skilled (notice I said "skilled" and not "mom-and-pop") groups will perform preventive maintenance that you could delay doing, thereby saving you substantially more money in the long run.

Upon achieving a level of income equivalent to that of your day job, you could, if you so choose, leave your day job. But keep in mind that if you resign too soon, you will experience financial stress and begin basing business decisions on where the next mortgage payment will come from rather than the long-term investment. Additionally, maintaining a job makes it significantly easier to purchase a home. It's easier to persuade a bank (or dealer) that you'll be able to make the installment payments if you can demonstrate that the money from the property you're purchasing is merely extra money, and that your regular employment pays most of your expenses.

How Your Credit Rating Influences Your Investments

Your FICO score is of vital importance to your real estate investing career. The range of purchaser FICO scores is between 300 and 850. You need to have a consistent FICO score; this will allow you to predict the level of financing for which you qualify. For example, if your FICO rating or FICO score is greater than 700, you are regarded as having premium credit and will qualify for the best rates and terms. With this exceedingly high FICO score, you will be eligible for low- or no-initial-installment loans, as well as payday advances.

If your credit score is in the 600s, you are considered to have excellent to good credit. It becomes marginally more difficult to acquire high credit-to-value (LTV) advances and to rely on express pay rather than complete documentation. When you have multiple investment properties, complete documentation of your income becomes increasingly cumbersome, as you must demonstrate all aspects of each pay property. You should make every effort to achieve and maintain a high FICO score in order to qualify for favorable insurance rates (more income!), higher loan-to-value proportions, complete documentation for all express pay sections, and generally more advantageous arrangements.

Credit Score and Credit-Affecting Factors

There are numerous variables that affect your FICO score. The three most important factors are your payment history, the amount and type of your current credit, and the percentage of your current credit that you are utilizing. Assuming you have a poor payment record, the only thing that will assist is time. If you pay your expenses on time, this portion of your credit score will gradually improve.

The amount and type of credit you have is also crucial. Lenders prefer to see some credit history, but an excess of retail store cards can lower your score. Finance organization advances are regarded as a last resort and have a greater negative impact on your credit score than other loans.

The last significant factor, and the one you can alter with the least amount of effort, is the credit limit on your current credit cards and credit extensions. This can alter quickly and has a substantial impact on your credit score.

When I was first starting out, my credit extensions and Visas were nearly or completely maxed out. My financial assessment increased from the middle 600s to the low-middle 700s after I paid off these debts of $5,000. This allowed me to obtain all the benefits of a higher FICO score, and all I had to do was focus on and pay off my existing Mastercard debt.

The importance of managing your Mastercard debt cannot be overstated. If your Mastercard is more than ninety percent utilized, you will be punished severely. Assuming you have multiple credit cards, pay them down so that no single card exceeds 90% and your total balances do not exceed 90% of your available credit.

Experian, TransUnion, and Equifax, the three largest consumer FICO rating agencies, prefer to see that you owe 30% or less of your total available credit. Consider that you have three Visas and owe $5,000. If your total available credit is only $5,000, you have a terrible credit score. You are pressed to the limit, resulting in a lower FICO score. But if your total available credit is $15,000, then you are only utilizing 30% of your available credit, which is excellent, and your credit score will increase.

Stop Handling Your Own Mess!

One of the greatest misconceptions about land contributing that frequently discourages individuals from contributing for themselves is the notion that investing in land requires a great deal of labor. Or, as I've recently alluded to, swinging the mallet.

When I first began researching land, I was convinced that the best way to invest was to find inspired merchants, organize deals, recover a property, place tenants, and then become the landowner of those tenants. It wasn't so much that I couldn't do any of them, but the prospect of each one sounded impossible to me. In retrospect, I recognize that this is the reason I initially avoided landing: I would have preferred to avoid doing so. I did not become an investor until I discovered alternative methods of putting money. These alternatives were considerably less labor-intensive.

To provide context for how remote investing can function, I will compare and contrast two distinct investment property investing methodologies. First, I'll explain the numerous approaches, and then we can discuss which one is preferable.

Investing in traditional rental properties

The conventional technique of investing in investment properties is referred to as a "esteem add" transaction. It is presently more frequently referred to as the "BRRRR model", where BRRRR stands for purchase recovery lease renegotiate revisit. You are purchasing a distressed property and then rehabilitating it to increase its overall value. When properly executed, the new value of the property as a result of your property development exceeds the amount you initially invested. It is comparable to flipping a property, except that the property is held and rented out instead of sold for a profit. But even if you keep the property, the value you've added is now part of the property's equity and your overall profit. The cycle of this strategy for purchasing investment properties would be as follows:

1. Locate a property. You can locate properties through a variety of sources. You can work with wholesalers, scour

the MLS frequently to find a good deal when it arises, and contact landowners to see if they are interested in selling... Occasionally, it requires being inventive.

2. Discuss the arrangement. When you find a deal you're interested in, you must work with the specialist or distributor to obtain all the necessary documents to close the transaction.

3. Finish up the arrangement. This requires collaborating with your bank, completing a property review, and completing a vast array of appropriate due diligence tasks.

4. Renovate the home. Start pounding your hammers!

5. Find occupants. You must advertise for tenants, process applications as they

come in, sign a lease with them, and then help them move in.

6. The landlord owns the property. You are taking support (and show) inquiries and resolving issues either by yourself or by employing project staff. You keep abreast of the current investment property laws in your area and ensure compliance with them. Eventually, you are responsible for both the resident and the property itself. In addition, if a resident needs to be removed, you're in charge of that procedure.

Investing in Turnkey Rental Properties

The concept behind a turnkey investment property, and the origin of its term, is that all you need to do is stick the key in the door, turn it, and you can begin earning income immediately. This would indicate that the property is lease-ready, requiring no recuperation, and that tenants are already in place and paying rent.

While the term 'turnkey' (also rendered 'turn-key' and 'turn-key') refers to the condition of a property, sometimes when people refer to investing in turnkey investment properties, they're actually purchasing these properties from legitimate turnkey organizations. These organizations, also known as comprehensive suppliers, seek out distressed properties, acquire them, and recover them.

Place occupants in the properties and establish a property management council for when the financial backer acquires the properties. Essentially, they are performing all of the previously mentioned "esteem add" labor. This implies that I, as the financial supporter, am not performing all of that task. In the absence of unforeseen circumstances, my contribution cycle would resemble the following:

1. Choose a property that I like. The turnkey providers provide me with a list of available inventory, and I choose the property I desire.

2. Sign the contract. Sign and return the document.

3. Do due industriousness. The principal advance—to ensure I am receiving the advertised property. The most important things are to obtain a property inspection and verify all the data.

4. Close on the real estate. Sign the final paperwork.

5. Supervise the property manager. This is inconsequential; it is merely to ensure that the property is proceeding as planned. As far as exertion is concerned, the worst-case scenario is that I may have to fire the property manager if they are not performing and hire another one, but I have never had to repair a toilet or interact with a tenant.

Do you observe a significant difference between the two occupations? The lists may appear to be of comparable length, but the scope of each of these means varies significantly between the two approaches. Compared to the turnkey model, the conventional model's level of responsibility is inherently more constrained.

You may wonder, based on these depictions, why anyone would do all the hard work if they can simply exceed everyone's expectations and have everything done for them.

It all comes down to statistics.

Comparing Traditional and Turnkey: the Numbers

With regard to private land, "market esteem" is the evident value of a property based on available information (such as current market interest and comparable properties). Using market value to evaluate conventional and turnkey strategies:

Traditional method: purchase property for substantially less than market value and then recover the property; these two costs should total less than the market value of the completed/improved property. Turnkey method: purchase completed/improved property at or near market value.

In the conventional approach, you stimulate appreciation by rehabilitating the property. Driving appreciation implies locating a run-down property, enhancing it in some way, and then selling it for more than you paid for it. This additional value is currently in your pocket, and you obtained it by "driving appreciation."

For example, if you purchase a distressed property for $50,000 and invest $20,000 in its recovery, your total investment in the property is $70,000. Following the recovery, the property is currently valued at $100,000. This is an additional $30,000 in value that now belongs to you because you limited the appreciation through the rehabilitation.

With a turnkey property, you are paying a market incentive for the property itself, and the property has been "improved," so you could not work on the property if necessary. Even if you could, you would have trouble selling it for significantly more than its market value. Due to the fact that you're purchasing a distressed property at a substantial discount to its market value, you have the opportunity to restore it, drive its appreciation, and sell it at its then-market value while still having the option to retain profits.

l yourself appear to be the superior option then? The So then is not adequate.

Why would anyone purchase a turnkey as opposed to placing work into a property themselves, given that the traditional method yields significantly higher returns?

We are now at the substance of this discussion.

Pay More for Less Work, or Work More for Greater Returns?

The majority of participants in this discussion are in favor of increasing returns by putting in more effort. There is a reason why people believe this is the best method to succeed in land contributing: it works. It does not, however, imply that hands-off strategies are ineffective.

The most common argument against keyless is that doing everything yourself saves money. This manifests itself in two crucial aspects of investment properties: getting a good deal on the property purchase itself by having the option to purchase a distressed property well below market value, and saving money by managing the property yourself rather than paying a property manager to do so. However, are you actually saving money by performing these tasks on your own? It depends on one's point of view.

Let's use property costs incurred by the board to investigate this. Typically, a property manager will charge the landowner 10% of the monthly lease as a fee for managing the property. Assuming that your investment property generates $1,000 per month in rental income, the executive's property expense would be $100 per month. When it comes to monthly income, every $100 matters because you typically receive only a few to two or three hundred dollars per month. Therefore, it is a good notion that people believe they can save $100 per month by acting as landlords.

If being a landlord is simple or enjoyable for you and does not have a negative impact on your happiness, there is no need to hire a property manager and you can keep the $100/month. In any case, there are a few factors that investors should consider when deciding whether to become landlords:

What is the value of your personal time?

How much time and effort is involved in being a landlord?

Say I value my time at $75 per hour. Therefore, if I took care of someone's business, I would charge them $75 per hour. If a property manager charges me $100 per month to manage my properties, how does this compare to the value of my time?

If my hourly rate is $75, I would need to work 1.34 hours to earn $100. If I spent 1.34 hours per month managing my investment property, I would incur the same expense as if I paid the property manager. Assuming I spent less than 1.34 hours per month conducting landowner duties, it would cost me less than $100, indicating that it would be financially advantageous for me to be the property manager. But if being a landlord consumed more than 1.34 hours of my time per month, which is worth more than $100, it would be financially advantageous to pay the property director $100 and not take the necessary steps myself.

Does the ownership of a property necessitate more than 1.34 hours per month? Overall, this is dependent upon the property and its inhabitants. Do you have a low-quality property that requires numerous repairs or tenants who are perpetually in need of something, breaking something, or not paying the rent? Or do you have low-maintenance tenants and low-maintenance properties, which require minimal time to maintain? Also, keep in mind that some months may require zero hours of your time, whereas others may require several hours. What will the typical duration be?

This is a true story that took place on one of my properties. During the time I was engaged in land investment in Nicaragua, I traveled there frequently. I had also begun purchasing rental properties, which were all managed by property managers. I was sitting in the resort pool with a pia colada in my hand (admittedly, it wasn't the first of the day) when I received a message from my property manager in Atlanta informing me that a storm had just passed through and damaged the roof of one of my properties. I told him to wait while I called my insurance company. I called the insurance company, pia colada still nearby, opened a claim, and gave them my property manager's contact information so their agent could contact him to arrange a site visit to assess the damage. I rang up with them, then sent my property manager a message informing him that the case had been documented and that the agent would contact him. He expressed his profound appreciation, and that was the end of the conversation. Apart from approving the final work proposal, I never did anything else regarding that rooftop because the property manager handled everything with the insurance company and the contractors.

I did not have to leave the pool or set down my pia colada when the roof of my house was blown off by a storm. I'm not certain what that would have meant for my excursion if I had been the landowner at that time. I do not know if I would have immediately boarded a plane or if I could have hired someone from abroad to inspect it. But I do know that, at a minimum, my roof-related to-do list would have included the following:

Communicate with tenants about temporary solutions and then again when contractors will be working.

coordinate with the adjuster

assemble at the property with the insurance adjuster.

locate a contractor for the project

oversee the contractor who carried out the task

How many hours would this have taken in total? I cannot really comprehend. Nevertheless, I am aware that it took me longer than the five minutes I spent in the pool to coordinate all of that effort.

In addition to exchanging my time for money, there is a further thought underlying all of this. What can be said about the third form of wealth, mental health? Stop worrying about how much time I would have needed to manage the top of this property and escaping Nicaragua to do it; however, compare the anxiety of managing and all of that to remaining in the pool and not stressing about it.

I recognize that the disadvantage to my mental health when I'm a landlord is not worth keeping an extra $100 per month in my ledger. Certain individuals, on the other hand, do not worry about landlording responsibilities and believe that the work justifies retaining the extra $100 in their ledgers every month with no mental impact. This will also be the case when examining more extensive giving procedures; some people won't mind and may even enjoy doing everything, while others won't. It is not necessary to focus on which course you choose; rather, it is important to comprehend your options and choose the one that best fits you. As each financial backer and circumstance will be unique, each financial backer must evaluate the financial and personal gratification arrangements for themselves.

The problem is that a large number of individuals are unaware that they can still provide financial support without exerting so much effort. It is something that all of these how-to guides have thankfully avoided.

There are additional factors to consider when deciding whether you should perform all the labor on your properties yourself or not.

The Future Requires A Benchmark Standard

As we write these lines, imagining a metaverse in one of its many manifestations seems straightforward, but it is extremely difficult to outline realistic assumptions that would allow us to recognize it as an Internet-like phenomenon, let alone consider it its successor.

It is much simpler to explain why a single-reference metaverse does not exist than to describe what it could be. There are numerous reasons why it is currently not feasible, beginning with the immaturity of the enabling technologies, which restricts the field of investigation to hypotheses and suggestions.

When we read reports stating that the metaverse business will be worth x or y billion dollars in 2025, we are well aware that they are referring to the path currently being pursued, which consists of numerous individual branded metaverses, autonomous 3D virtual worlds where companies will find fertile ground to expand their businesses related to new digital experiences. To date, however, the conditions for interconnecting this assortment of metaverses appear hazy.

To create the metaverse with a capital M, which is intended to be the only multiverse capable of comprehending the multitude of individual metaverses, it would first be necessary to establish a common consortium, similar to how the W3C was established in 1994 to oversee the regulation of Internet network services. A super body capable of defining standards, communication protocols, and all the necessary aspects to ensure the correct interoperability of the services themselves, allowing anyone to access the global web.

No one could have foreseen that the Internet would carry us to where we are today, completely upending social and economic models on a global scale, thirty years ago, when it was in everyone's best interest to foster the growth of new businesses.

The pioneering momentum of the web's infancy has progressively given way to dominant positions, where big tech is keenly interested in developing new business platforms without jeopardizing their hegemony. Governments start late once again, as technology always advances quicker than regulations.

It will require a concerted effort by governments, developer institutions, and technology titans to immediately establish a fundamental condition of equilibrium so that the metaverse becomes, for everyone, a real opportunity for development as well as the actualization of the dystopian scenarios described in science fiction.

CHAPITRE IV

Investment Funds

You are not investing on your own in an asset. There is a pool of investors who contribute money to an aggregate investment.

It is a safer option than purchasing stocks because you are not bearing the risk on your own.

By utilizing an asset, you have access to a greater number of investment opportunities, more administration expertise to assist you, and reduced investment costs than if you were investing on your own.

You do not make individual decisions regarding how the asset's resources should be allocated. You choose an asset based on its objectives, risk, and expenses.

A manager of the asset determines which protections it should hold, in what quantities, and when the protections should be traded. Consequently, you benefit from superior administrative expertise.

You are acquiring shares of this asset. The majority of assets have a specific theme:

- Geographical

- Industrialization

- Varieties of investments

- Size of the firm

There are also numerous types of funds:

- Mutual funds

- Index funds

- Exchange-exchanged funds

- Money market funds

- Hedge funds

The advantages of venture reserves include:

They carry various items.

- Easy to store away

- A professional cashier is required for the shipment.

- Low acquisition cost

The disadvantages are:

- The costs

- Performance or rate of return are not assured.

- You cannot change your investment because the asset manager has control.

You should contribute for a minimum of five years. If you anticipate needing immediate access to your funds, then this may not be the best investment for you.

Utilizing an asset grocery store or stages is the most cost-effective method for depositing funds into reserves. They are available online.

Investing in reserves involves two stages. Initially, you must determine which platform you will use; then, you must decide which project to incorporate.

You will incur fees for both using the platform and purchasing the funds.

Mutual Funds

A shared asset is an asset type. They are investment vehicles that allow you to merge your funds with those of other investors to purchase a variety of stocks, securities, and other investments.

Notably, a financial supporter of a common asset does not possess the protections to which the asset contributes; they only own portions of the asset itself.

You may trade your asset shares once per day at the close of the market for all shared assets. The price fluctuates based on the value of the asset's components at the end of each business day.

You can earn money in three possible ways:

- Income derived from share dividends

- Coupon on bonds

- A rise in the price of protections. If the asset share price is

If the fund grows, you can sell your shares for a profit. There are four types of common funds:

- Those who invest capital in shares (value reserves). They invest in corporate proposals by purchasing shares of a variety of publicly traded companies. They have a greater development potential, but experience cost fluctuations.

- Bonds (fixed-remuneration reserves). The most popular type of fixed pay common assets. Financial supporters are repaid a reasonable amount for their investment in the enterprise. The securities reserve invests in government and corporate debt. They are viewed as a more secure investment than stocks but have less growth potential than value funds.These reserves are frequently well-managed and seek to purchase somewhat undervalued securities to sell for a profit.

•Money market (transient obligation). It consists of secure short-term obligations, typically government Treasury bills. This is a secure location to store your currency. You will not receive substantial returns, but you will not need to worry about losing your initial investment. The average return is somewhat greater than the amount you would obtain from a standard checking or investment account.

- Stocks and bonds. The objective is to reduce risk by investing in both.

diversifying.

- Income reserve. Consistently, they generate current income. These assets are primarily invested in government and high-quality corporate debt, retaining these securities until development generates interest payments. Consequently, they are longer range. However, their primary objective is to generate a steady income for their financial supporters. Common financial supporters are moderate, retired individuals. Charge-aware financial supporters may want to steer clear of these funds because they generate standard pay.

Each common asset is designed to mitigate risk while capturing business sector gains.

The benefits of mutual funds:

• You gain the benefit of having an expert supervisor continuously evaluate your portfolio.

• The cost of the exchange is divided among all investors in the asset, reducing the cost per investor.

• Mutual assets invest in a wide spectrum of areas, immediately differentiating the portfolio.

The obstacles are:

• Costly fees

• Fiscal inefficacy

- inadequate exchange execution

- Possibility of board abuse

Mutual assets may be acquired directly from a shared asset organization, a bank, or a financial institution. Before making a donation, you should create an account.

There are a variety of costs that may be associated with common funds.

Some assets are accompanied by exchange fees or commissions for trading. Annual asset operating expenses are a yearly proportion of the managed assets.

Some assets incur a recovery cost if you sell shares you've only held for a brief duration.

As with any endeavor, there are also risks involved. There is always a possibility that the value of your common asset will decline. Mutual assets are typically more appropriate for long-term investors.

If you anticipate needing your funds shortly, a mutual fund may not be the best choice. This is because the return in that amount of time (after deducting the cost of fees) may not be sufficient to make the investment worthwhile.

Index Funds

A record store is a business that monitors a market file (for example, the S&P 500, the top 500 stocks in the United States).

Typically, they consist of equities or bonds. There is a record and a list reserve for virtually every financial market in existence.

The superintendent of assets constructs a portfolio whose assets reflect the protections of a particular index.

It attempts to replicate the development and execution of a financial market program. It means to match rather than surpass its

performance.

It is similar to a shared or trade-exchanged asset.

(ETF). To spend:

Choose the file. There are numerous files that can be followed using file reserves.

You can also view area records associated with specific businesses, country files that target equities in single countries, and style files that highlight rapidly growing companies.

• Select a fund

• Buy stocks

The advantages are:

• Broad market openness. There are file archives accessible for a variety of endeavors. Stock record assets and security list funds are available for purchase.

• Low operating expenses. They have a reduced proportion of board costs. The administrator of record subsidizes property exchanges less frequently, resulting in lower exchange fees and commissions.

• Low portfolio liquidity

You can contribute with reduced risk. Most accounts contain dozens or even hundreds of stocks and other investments, and the increase in diversification makes you more resistant to significant losses.

• Since they employ a hands-off approach to investment, they incur lower costs and fees than actively managed reserves. The file store manager must acquire the securities or other interests in a file. He is not required to identify specific performing securities.

• You will incur fewer expenses. In comparison to numerous other investments, they have a high rate of return.

These are the obstacles to a record store speculation:

• You will never outperform the market. They are designed to mirror the performance of the market.

• You have no misfortune protection. When the market plummets, your list asset will plummet as well, as list assets follow their respective business sectors through a variety of difficulties.

• You will not own your favorite stocks eternally.

• No authority over holdings

Generally, the speculation will be conducted over an extended period of time to stimulate positive performance.

Investors make an initial minimum investment ($3,000 - $10,000) and pay annual expenses to maintain the asset (a small proportion of the capital invested).

You can purchase a list reserve directly from a common asset organization or a financial institution. To purchase shares in your preferred list store, you can establish an account directly with the common asset organization offering the fund.

Exchange-Traded Funds (ETFs)

It is a collection of businesses that are sold on a market. Similar to individual equities, ETF shares are traded throughout the day at prices that fluctuate based on supply and demand.

The asset supplier claims the resources, designs an asset to follow their presentation, and then solicits investors for stakes in that asset.

Shareholders own a portion of an ETF, but they do not own the underlying assets.

The primary distinction between ETFs and common assets is that ETF shares trade throughout the trading day, whereas shares of mutual funds only trade once a day after the market closes.

ETFs have become ubiquitous investments. Due to their many benefits, including low cost proportions, liquidity, venture scope, and a low speculation threshold, they are ideal for beginning investors.

Types of exchange-traded funds:

• Bond. It may include government, corporate, and civil securities. Security ETFs detest individual internet-based securities because they lack a maturity date, so their most common use is to produce recurring cash payments to the financial backer. These payments are derived from the interest generated by the individual securities within the fund.

• Businesses. Observe a particular industry

• Products. Invest in commodities such as crude petroleum or gold

The monetary system. Put resources into unfamiliar currencies

A trade-exchanged asset has a price that facilitates its purchase and sale.

You can have an actively managed ETF where portfolio managers are more involved with trading portions of companies; however, an actively managed asset will have higher expenses than an inactively managed asset.

Benefits of ETFs:

• They provide investors with the ability to acquire as stock prices rise and decline

• Investors can benefit from dividend-paying companies.

• Investors in ETFs are eligible for a portion of the earnings

- Flexible. During the day, when business sectors are accessible, ETFs are traded.

- They provide diversification for a portfolio

- Lower price. They are passively due, with significantly reduced cost ratios compared to funds that are actively managed.

- Tax benefits. Due to underlying differences, shared assets incur higher capital charges than ETFs. They have smaller capital additions and are payable upon the ETF's issuance.

Disadvantages of ETFs:

- Subject to display variation

• Subject to administrative expenses and other costs

• The cost could be greater. Assuming that you compare ETFs and investing in a specific stock,

inventory expenses are higher

ETFs are traded through online specialists and traditional representative dealers. You must establish a corporate account.

Money Market Funds

It is a type of common asset that invests in extremely liquid, short-term instruments. They are expected to provide investors with a high degree of dissolvability and an exceedingly low degree of risk.

A venture store company supports the conjecture that is a currency market reserve.

A currency market reserve generates income but minimal capital appreciation, implying that the underlying investment appreciates minimally.

Money market accounts are a wise investment if you can maintain a high minimum balance, limit your withdrawals, and understand that you are not protected against inflation.

They are divided into the following categories:

- Prime liquid assets. Invests non-depository assets in floating-rate obligations and business paper.

The government's currency on hand. Contributes nearly 99.5% of its total assets to actual money and government securities.

• Government reserve. Invest in conventional US depository obligation securities

• Non-taxable cash store. Offer income exempt from U.S. taxation

The benefits of currency market funds are:

• Excellent location to stop currency for the present. Safer due to the fact that these types of assets invest in generally safe vehicles. Consistently generates a low single-digit

return for

investors.

• They invest in extremely fluid security measures. This indicates that financial backers can transfer them easily.

The obstacles are:

• Purchasing power is resilient. They can generate returns under expansion, resulting in diminished purchasing power.

• Fees can consume a substantial portion of the benefit. Usually, a minimum balance is required to avoid a monthly service fee.

• They are not protected by the government. In the event that the investment reserve company becomes bankrupt, you may lose all of your money.

- Low-priced premium

- Inflation danger

Generally, you should pay tax on the premium you receive or the profits generated by the assets as you acquire them. Unless they are held in a tax-exempt retirement account.

In contrast to certificates of deposit, currency market accounts can be closed at any time without penalty.

You can purchase currency market assets from investment firms, financial institutions, and banks.

Earnest Money Deposit Not Refundable

Jerry, who was brand-new to land contributing, was impatient to complete his first arrangement and had no desire to delay doing so. Jerry had been organizing with anyone and everyone and had somehow made it onto the email list of an out-of-state distributor. Eventually, he received an email from that distributor regarding a property that appeared to be the deal of the century. A house that, once thoroughly renovated, could be worth $130,000 was available for purchase for only $60,000. Jerry realized after examining the property that it should have been substantially remodeled, but his calculations indicated that there was still a tremendous potential gain in the arrangement. Jerry was ecstatic and thought to himself, "Observing an agreement is not as difficult as everyone says. Hell locate me with these extraordinary arrangements!"

In order to close a contract with the distributor, Jerry was required to provide a $3000 non-refundable cash deposit. The distributor assured him that it was standard for transactions with such a high probability of profit to require a 5% down payment prior to the execution of a contract. Jerry sent the check to the distributor, and after the agreement was signed by both parties, it was sent to a local closing company to prepare for the closing.

Jerry, meanwhile, desired to gain an early advantage on the project and dispatched a project worker to the property. In addition, he contacted a real estate agent to aid him in determining how much the property would be worth after repairs were completed, as well as what repairs would be required to fetch the highest price.

His enthusiasm waned when his agent informed him that it probably wouldn't sell for more than $100,000, regardless of its excellent condition. The potential value of $130,000 in Jerry's mind originated from the distributor. It was a price that his agent explained was unreasonable for the area in which the home was located. In addition, the hired laborer discovered a few issues that Jerry had overlooked, and the cost to renovate, even if they used the cheapest grade materials, was estimated to exceed $30,000. Suddenly, the arrangement didn't appear so good, and he considered dropping sponsorship.

He remained to risk losing $3,000 if he fled. Instead of leaving the money, he decided to buy the property. He financed the purchase with a home equity credit extension from his primary residence. He hired a replacement laborer who informed him that the job could be completed for under $30,000 without a doubt.

When the work appeared to be complete, he recruited an alternative specialist who suggested that listing the home for $124,900 would expedite its sale. However, after several months, the home remained unsold. Not a single proposal was submitted. The home's few appearances suggested that it required an excessive amount of maintenance. "A lot of work?" pondered Jerry. "How could the house possibly require more work?" It was simply renovated from top to bottom!"

Jerry fired his agent, citing her tardiness, lack of open houses, and failure to solicit bids from individuals who viewed the property. He began to blame the economy for his difficulties, complaining that the market in that region was lagging.

Meanwhile, the premium payments on his home equity credit extension were beginning to have a significant impact on his finances. Consequently, he planned to renegotiate his investment property and withdraw the funds used to renovate the home to repay the home equity line of credit.

Frustrated by the lack of buyers, he listed the property for lease and immediately received an enormous premium. He was relieved to finally have concrete information about this property.

As soon as the residents moved in, they began to report problems. There were numerous issues, ranging from paint removal to pipe leaks to electrical problems. It soon became apparent that the hired worker who had redesigned the house had made concessions wherever he went.

Jerry was incurring monthly losses due to maintenance issues. In the end, the tenants grew so weary of the problems that they stopped paying the rent. Jerry had to remove them, which cost him thousands of dollars more in lost rent, void mortgage payments, and legal fees.

When the house was finally abandoned, he had to hire a second worker to re-apply the paint, this time with a preliminary coat, as well as replace the floor coverings that the previous occupants had destroyed, and repair other issues that the first worker had caused.

Now, nearly a long time after the initial purchase, Jerry made the property available for purchase once more. This time, however, he was compelled to get rid of it and recoup his losses. Unfortunately for Jerry, the market had significantly declined, and properties were selling for less than when he purchased them. Until he finally received an offer for $90,000, he watched as the price of the property's renovations needed to decrease ever more.

Jerry determined that he had ultimately lost more than $23,000 and that the property had consumed significant portions of his life. Reflecting, he recalled what he could have done differently...

He could have accepted the $3,000 loss and withdrawn from the contract. It would have spared him over $20,000, years of his life, and enormous amounts of stress.

He may have hired his first employee despite the fact that he did not provide Jerry with the necessary information. In addition, he could have heeded the realtor's prediction that the property would not sell for more than $100,000. Jerry discovered that realtors who don't typically portray a rosy picture may provide the most trustworthy advice.

Instead of blaming the specialist, the economy, or the market, he could have simply reduced the asking price from $124,900 to a level that would have generated an offer.

Instead of renegotiating, which resulted in tens of thousands of dollars in additional fees and costs, he could have recently sold the property by reducing the disrepair cost in order to release his home equity line of credit.

Rather than relying on leasing a property that wouldn't sell, he should have determined why it wasn't selling and resolved that issue, as opposed to creating a new and more serious one.

Even better, he could not have agreed to non-refundable sincere cash. Perhaps he could have arranged seven days for due diligence so he wouldn't have had to risk losing $3,000 to begin with?

This tale has been told numerous times. Everything began with the acceptance of non-refundable genuine cash with no innovation period. But that was only the beginning, as this error was not the most consequential decision that led to the remainder of the problems. Ultimately,

Jerry's biggest mistake was overpaying for the property.

When someone pays a high price for a property, it spreads out over a vast area like a pebble cast into a still lake. There is not enough money in the budget to pay a quality project worker, so the work is performed poorly to meet the budget constraints. The property should then be recorded higher than it should be to compensate for the high purchase price. Then, when it fails to sell, the listing agent is held accountable.

Sadly, if a buyer purchases a property that has been inadequately renovated (to compensate for the financial backer paying excessively), the buyer is purchasing a home with concealed issues that may not reappear for months or years after moving in. In this model, Jerry had to sleep in the bed he had made by assuming responsibility for any maintenance concerns.

In the end, the real culprit should be the irrational financial supporter who overpaid for the property and set in motion the cascading effect.

Two Lost Transactionscaper

Ben was eager to compose his first composition. He had read as many books as he could get his hands on, attended every class that came to town, read online articles and watched videos for hours every day, and spent his entire life investing in courses and trainings. Along his travels, he encountered Victor, a financial backer who was also a hard currency bank. Ben found exceptional deals but lacked the financial wherewithal to purchase them. Victor appeared to be such a kind-hearted individual because he offered to help individuals in Ben's situation.

Ben tried for many months to implement what he had learned about observing great arrangements, but he continued to pursue awful arrangement terrible arrangement. Ben reasoned, "Observing arrangements is MUCH more difficult than they claim." Ben, however, was not a quitter, so he persisted. After nearly 9 months, he finally felt he had discovered a bargain of the century. The seller was desperate to sell the property because he was heading to jail and did not want to continue making mortgage payments while he was incarcerated. Prior to making a proposal, Ben needed to ensure he had the financial resources to purchase the item, so he approached Victor for assistance with subsidizing the deal. After Ben provided as much information as he likely knew about the arrangement, including the contact information of the vendor to inspect the home, Victor gave him the green light to finance the arrangement up to $150,000.

Ben made an offer of $150,000, and the dealer asked if he could consider it. The merchant had been difficult to reach, making arrangements at the last minute before disappearing for some time. Amazingly, the next day the merchant informed him that he had decided to offer to a different financial supporter who offered him more. Ben was devastated. All that time and effort had culminated in this one agreement, which was subsequently snatched away by another investor.

Ben contemplated whether he ought to continue with land contributing. Perhaps it wasn't truly intended for him. He realized that the uncommon route would not have been easy and there would have been bumps and injuries along the way, so he resolved to proceed. He also found some solace in the fact that the first deal he lost was a good one because it was taken by another player. He now knew what a champion looked like, and if he did it once, he could do it again. Three more months of arduous labor passed before he discovered a potentially extraordinary arrangement. This time, however, he planned to close the deal promptly and not waste any time. He made the proposal to the vendor, but the vendor required a suitable window of time to carefully consider it. Ben contacted Victor while he awaited a response and obtained information about financing this arrangement. Ben was thrilled to receive Victor's approval to finance the project. Unfortunately for Ben, the vendor stopped returning his calls and messages. The dealer had fundamentally disappeared.

Ben was completely demoralized. This was his second authentic arrangement in nine months of arduous labor, and he had missed it. Although this issue appeared to be a variant, the merchant had simply vanished.

As diligent as Ben was, he was also having trouble explaining to his loved ones why it was prudent for him to continue doing something that, after almost a year of squandering his time, energy, and money, had produced no results. In fact, his father mentioned that if Ben had spent all that time working at McDonald's instead of dabbling with land, he would have amassed a great deal of money (instead of spending thousands on courses and trainings). It was a hard pill for Ben to swallow. However much he despised abandoning his fantasy about being a land financial backer, he believed he had done as well as he possibly can and it simply didn't work out for him.

A couple of months after the fact, recollecting over his short vocation in land contributing, he pondered whatever happened to those two extraordinary arrangements he had found. After conducting some Internet research, he discovered that a similar LLC had acquired them both and subsequently sold them for several thousand dollars more. It was unbelievably excruciating to see firsthand that he was so close to making a substantial amount of money, but someone else had won the money. Who was the entity's founder? He investigated who this privileged financial backer who owned this LLC was, and nearly fell out of his chair when he saw the name... Victor! He was scarcely able to handle it. The hard cash bank had taken both of those arrangements from him!

Victor provided Ben with an obsolete illustration of how genuine land contribution functions. Extraordinary arrangements are exceedingly hard to obtain, and if they are not completely secured, they can be easily stolen. Local financial backers who posture themselves as hard cash moneylenders are notorious for accepting agreements from wholesalers who do not have their agreements secured. Vendors are neither biased nor unwavering; they will sell to whoever can pay them the most money the quickest. In both of Ben's transactions, Victor was aware of the deal and location, went to the property, and made a slightly higher offer than Ben.

Ben felt betrayed by Victor and disturbed by the land in general. If that's what the real estate business was like, he thought, then he wanted nothing to do with it anymore. Ben never again ventured into the realm of real estate investment.

Most deplorable for Ben was that had he gotten those two arrangements secured with the right desk work prior to connecting for subsidizing, he would have made a huge measure of cash. Furthermore, from those two starting arrangements, may have turned into a deep rooted, extremely effective land financial backer. However, he failed to perceive the lessons, which irrevocably altered the course of his real estate career.

Effective and Beneficial Learning Lessons

(1)Excellent provisions are difficult to locate. Utilize them when you discover them.

(2) When you have a great bargain, secure it with a contract and, if

possible, a recorded instrument to ensure that no one can take it from you. Then, you can seek for cash to purchase the item.

(3) Do not abandon land, regardless of the presence of temporary obstacles. The underlying examples you acquire from your errors can serve as the foundation for a prosperous business career.

Investors With A High Net Worth Versus Small Investors

This investor is perpetually anxious to make a profit. So many of them want to earn $50,000 per month by investing $500,000, as I have observed. Obsession with winning is a proven indication that one will inevitably fail. He always overpays because he does not comprehend the value. He is unaware of the importance of compounding. In this market, a person without knowledge of compounding cannot earn money.

Whoever comprehends interest earns it. Whoever does not comprehend interest, pays it.

Rich and wealthy investors always look to the market to speak and signal when to buy, whereas this poor man wants the market to behave according to his preferences.

Have you observed a tiny investor or trader buying positions on the market? His eyes are on the terminal, anticipating a price increase. And if it neither rises nor falls, he murmurs, "Go, go up. Why aren't you ascending?" This is true.

People develop a fixation on the market and market rates. In contrast, an investor with a high net worth is exempt from such concerns. He eats, drinks, and spends his days enjoying life.

The market is king. It is comparable to a mother with two sons. One is a wealthy investor and the other is an impoverished individual. For a mother, the two males are identical. Market accords them the same consideration. Same platform for trading, nearly the same brokerage, and playing regulations of the market, this market cannot assist more than by providing equal opportunities to all market participants. The impoverished investor has his own difficulties. He must pay the EMI on his mortgage, his children's tuition, his household expenditures, etc. He has only one goal in view, which is to profit from this market. He is hurrying. Consequently, he loses his mind, begins to fantasize and daydream, becomes entangled in his own senseless schemes, and loses all of his money on the market.

When there are no exceptional values available, the affluent investor waits. He is able to endure. He receives daily, weekly, and monthly income from his other sources. The wealthy investor understands what he wants and is patient enough to wait months or even years for his next investment opportunity.

Little man is up to his ears in debt. As a consequence, he is constantly perspiring in order to make payments on his house, refrigerator, car, and credit cards. He is impatient and perpetually frustrated. He tells himself he must make money quickly. And he wishes for "huge, juicy megabucks." In the end, the little man loses money in the stock market, gambles it away, or fritters it away on senseless schemes. This "money nerd" spends his entire existence racing up the financial escalator.

However, the irony is as follows. If the little guy had adopted a strict policy of never spending more than he earned, as well as spending less than he had, and invested his extra savings in intelligent, income-producing securities, he would have daily, weekly, and monthly income just like the wealthy man. Instead of becoming a pitiful loser, the little man would have been a financial victor.

Therefore, this poor investor must first understand the value of compounding and employ a rational approach to avoiding overspending. He must adopt the mindset of a High Net Worth Investor. What if he lacks significant wealth? In proportion to the HNI's wealth, he can invest and trade with his own funds. He must comprehend the worth of the money. He must develop patience and act at the appropriate time, and then he will receive money like a wealthy investor.

Tips for Women Unafraid of Venturing into the Unknown!

As you pursue your own desires, here are a few suggestions that have aided me in my own path to advancement. Wherever your fantasies drive you, do not hesitate to venture into the uncharted world. I wish you success and contentment on your voyage!

Imagine your ideal existence. Try not to limit your aspirations due to a lack of resources, skills, money, organization, or other factors that make progress appear improbable.

Plan your fantasyland existence. You should have a reason more compelling than the inconvenience you will encounter on the trip! Include your vision and an explanation of why your desires are worth pursuing. Peruse them daily and take action on a consistent basis to make your vision a reality.

Develop the self-assurance and coarseness to pursue your ambitions with tenacity no matter what! Life's adversities can derail even the greatest of achievements. When the pony throws you off and you fall out of the seat, pull up your young lady undergarments and remount.

Choose optimism when you feel despondent! Recognize that each obstacle will make you more grounded and intelligent. Accept that everything will be fine. Invoke God in order for God to strengthen and direct you. Although emotions fluctuate, mentality is a choice!

Consider that you have the means to address each challenge. Start by pondering, "How might I?" Continue conceptualizing and evaluating potential solutions until you have determined the best course of action for each problem.

Develop a network of emotional support! Get authentic and helpless. Nobody among us has everything figured out. Be sufficiently unassuming to solicit guidance and support from your peers and coaches. If you lack support, you should contemplate joining a mastermind.

Master your time and money, or your time and money will master you! Schedule your day and only complete tasks that can be accommodated by your schedule. Include time for coping with yourself and your closest loved ones. Learn how to budget, save, take care of obligations, and most importantly, increase your income.

Give yourself style! Praise little successes. They will propel you forward. Set aside a few minutes for you, since you are significant! Forgive yourself when you battle and make mistakes. You are an impressive and courageous woman, but you are not the legendary Wonder Woman. She does not juggle nearly as many ropes as we do!

Three Genuine Currencies

We exchange money for necessities. If I need an apple, I will exchange money for it. As I am in need of a home, I am willing to exchange money for one. If someone desires one of my items, they can pay me money in exchange.

As its name implies, money signifies "usefulness." In the aforementioned instances, cash is available for use as a medium of exchange. Assuming that cash merely denotes "usable," is cash the only thing that can be considered a currency?

Most people probably consider money when they consider a currency. But when I consider everything I do on a daily basis, I realize that money is not the only form of currency I employ. In fact, it is not even my primary source of funds. On any given day, I am likely to give or receive any of the following monetary forms, or a combination of them:

1. money

2. time

3. equilibrium

Similarly to how I give cash in exchange for something, I can also give my time in exchange for something. I may also be forced to give up a portion of my mental stability in exchange for something.

Consider that I need custom shelves for my family room. I have two options for having these stands constructed:

1. I will hire someone to construct them.

2. Construct them myself.

Regarding this type of circumstance, the majority of individuals center their attention on money. The typical argument against employing someone for any task is the money that can be saved by not employing the individual. In light of this argument, I conclude that I should save the money I would spend on a third party and construct the cabinets myself.

Regarding the construction of cabinets, I have two or three considerations. First of all, I have no idea how to construct frames. In addition, I am not naturally gifted at that type of task. As I've mentioned previously, I'm not overly intelligent, so figuring out how to construct them would likely not come easily or naturally to me. The subsequent thought is that I do not particularly enjoy worrying about things I am poor at and dislike. A third thought is that since books are heavy, if I don't assemble the racks precisely I risk the entire rack collapsing and a section of the divider detaching when I load it with books.

Consequently, it is evident that if I construct the shelves myself, I will pay for them with my time and my mental acuity. The time component would be a reality for anyone building something on their own, and the mental acuity component would be obvious to me and anyone else who has absolutely no interest in or natural aptitude for that type of work. Consequently, while I just saved the money I would have paid someone else to assemble the racks, I paid for the racks with two lesser-known monetary units: time and sanity.

When I was around 13 years old, I believed I needed to earn a billion dollars when I grew up. It seemed like a great personal challenge to determine a means to get that going. Throughout school, I clung to the goal of amassing substantial wealth, and the notion played a significant role in my underlying career decisions. However, it wasn't until I became an entrepreneur that I began to alter my priorities.

As soon as I had what I had previously referred to as a 'lifestyle plan' and business, my time and mental health became much more important in my daily life, taking precedence over money. I realized that I would prefer not to earn a gazillion dollars if it meant not devoting the totality of my time and mental acuity to what I was doing. While I was initially enthralled by the prospect of making a billion dollars, and I certainly wouldn't say anything negative if that occurs in the future, I realized that I'm not willing to sacrifice my time (for sleeping, snowboarding, and lounging by the ocean) and my mental stability (for everything blissful) for that amount of money.

This implies that my time and mental health are more valuable to me than money. Consequently, it may be more economical for me to pay more for something than for me to save the money and do it on my own. Do you understand?

If I were to rank every cash—money, time, and mental stability—according to their importance to me, my list would appear as follows:

1. equilibrium

2. time

3. money

Mental stability is my most valued commodity. Time is my second most valued commodity, and both are more important to me than money. Your list may appear to be different from mine, but that is how I rank the financial criteria for myself.

When I ask myself, "What is the least expensive way for me to complete this task or acquire this item? ", I am compelling myself to assign a value to each form of money so I can more precisely weigh my least expensive option. While cash is obviously my least expensive option, there are times when I wouldn't mind investing the effort in a task if it doesn't cost me my mental stability. In such situations, I might expend some of my energy to save money.

Occasionally, it may be acceptable for me to pay less for something that required more effort, provided that doing so does not compromise my mental health. The important aspect is not so much where I save money, but rather knowing precisely what I'm investing in.

Numerous individuals never consider that they are expending mental or physical strength on something.

Rarely can you purchase something or have something performed without spending at least one of the monetary standards. Which form of currency is more expensive for you? The answer to this question will be different for each individual, as well as for various duties or purchases. Flipping a home would cost me not only significant amounts of time and mental health, both of which are essential to me. To preserve my time and sanity, it is therefore preferable for me to pay with cash for a more expensive lease-ready investment property. For some individuals, flipping a house may not only come effortlessly, but also bring them pleasure.

Considered as a whole, it is prudent to set aside money rather than time and rationality.

How would you evaluate the three financial benchmarks? Make number one the money you value the most, i.e., your most expensive money. The third amount of money should be the least essential to you, i.e., it should be the least expensive. You can demonstrate here:

#1 #2 #3

Once you have determined which monetary forms are most important to you, be sure to keep them in mind when making decisions in land placing and throughout your daily life. You'll be amazed at how much more amenable things become when they align with your priorities.

Shares/Stocks/Equities

Although they are comparative terms, there are distinctions between them.

The term stocks is more inclusive. It represents a share of ownership. Typically, shares represent a portion of responsibility for a particular company.

Stocks are divided into shares; the smallest division of a company's stock is a share. Every share of stock represents an offer to invest in a company. For instance, if a person claims 1% of a company's stock, you can say they have 1% of the company's offer.

Equity represents ownership of an organization's assets minus its liabilities. Stocks are small units issued by a company that can be bought and traded.

Why do companies provide them? It allows them to raise funds and locate investors.

When you acquire an offer, you acquire a stake in a company and become a shareholder.

You may have a few privileges and benefits as an investor. You could, for instance, deliberate on business matters or receive profit payments.

The dividend payment is a portion of the advantages paid to investors by a company. A company is not required to generate profits. They can be paid on a recurring basis or as a one-time payment.

Shares do not provide a guarantee of profit, and there is risk associated with all investments. Costs may rise or fall.

You can purchase shares on your own or merge your funds with others in a joint venture. This is referred to as a fund.

How long would it be prudent for you to make contributions? Preferably, a considerable amount of time to allow for the passage of time in case you incur a loss due to market fluctuations.

If you can't hold off your cash for that long and require access to it sooner, then offers are probably not the best option for you at this time.

According to the idiom, do not lock up your assets in one location. It is too risky to hold stock in a single company, and if the value of an investment falls, you will lose money.

What are the advantages of stocks?

- You could potentially receive dividends
- They can cover costs • Adaptable

What are the disadvantages of stocks?

- You probably won't get dividends
- Risky
- Market cost can fluctuate

As a first-time investor, a safe option for you would be to invest in a stocks&shares Isas. An Isa is a single bank account with securities and dividends. Isas allow you to invest in a variety of investments and funds.

An Isa is the British equivalent of the American IRA.

You can grow your money in two ways with an offer: if the price of the offer increases, you can generate a profit (it will be worth more than when you purchased it), and if the company decides to pay you dividends.

The easiest method to acquire shares is through an online offer management platform. You are able to purchase shares from any company listed on the stock exchange.

You ought to establish a trading account. After opening and funding your account, you are able to purchase equities through the dealer's website.

Other alternatives include using a full-service stockbroker or purchasing shares directly from the company.

How would you select stocks? An excellent place to start is by researching companies you have interacted with as a customer.

What quantity of deals would you be wise to acquire? The overwhelming majority may anticipate holding between ten and twenty stocks.

If you wish to purchase from the London Stock Exchange or the New York Stock Exchange, an intermediary is required. Additionally, they will charge you a fee and frequently work on commission.

What does an offer cost? It fluctuates in response to market demand from buyers and sellers. If demand is significant, costs will also increase.

There are several fees you should be aware of:

• Account fees. This may be delayed depending on the number of trades you conduct.

• Inactivity fees. This could be assessed if your account exceeds the predetermined minimum number of transactions. Because they want you to remain with them, relatively few businesses impose this fee at present.

- Buying or selling. Each time you exchange shares, a fee is assessed.

- Stamp obligation. When purchasing shares, you typically pay a 0.5% transaction fee to the exchange. The only party responsible for payment is the purchaser.

Dividend Investing

This is a method for purchasing dividend-paying securities in order to profit from your investments.

Dividends are payments made by a partnership to its investors. When you own securities that generate profits, you receive a portion of the organization's earnings.

If the company you own stock in has a profit reinvestment plan, you can choose to have your profits reinvested to purchase additional shares rather than receiving them as a dividend.

Regular profit pay is a reliable and secure method of building a nest fund.

Companies that pay out 60% or less of their income as profits are generally safer investments because they are predictable.

Consider organizations that have a history of stable pay and cash flow.

The majority of pay from profits is taxed as common pay, but qualified profit equities held for a longer period (at least 60 days) are taxed at the lower capital increases charge rates.

Bonds

This is the juncture at which a credit is made to an organization or the government. They will provide securities when they need to raise funds to support initiatives.

The primary distinction between a security and a credit is that a security can be traded. There is usually a market where they can be traded. Credits are typically non-transferable arrangements between institutions and customers.

Bonds charge loan fees. The loan fees may be variable or fixed. A security has an expiration date, and when that date arrives, you should receive your money in full.

What is the bond's cost? • The creditworthiness of the person or entity providing the security. The bond is more hazardous the lower its rating. Continuously evaluate the guarantor's track record to determine if they are dependable or hazardous.

• The time remaining until maturity • The interest rate

You can present the attachment to various financial supporters. You are not required to remain with it until its expiration date.

What benefits do bonds offer?

• You are compensated with revenue payments • You receive all the money you contributed if you remain until the end • You can sell it for a profit

What are the downsides?

• Companies can default on their payments to you • If the financing cost decreases, so does the amount of your return

You may observe a security with a higher loan fee, but this indicates that the default risk is higher the higher the financing cost.

Avoid contributing solely based on the advertised financing cost. If the loan fee is high, it indicates the securities are riskier, and you have a greater chance of losing your entire investment.

When financing costs increase, bond prices decline, and vice versa. The loan cost hazard occurs when anticipated interest rates fluctuate. In the event that the loan rate rises, you will be left with a security returning below market rates.

The greater the potential for development, the greater the possibility that interest rates will increase.

There are two methods for generating income by investing in bonds.

The first option is to retain these securities until their maturity date and collect revenue installments. Typically, security premiums are paid twice per year.

The subsequent step is to sell them for a higher price than you initially paid.

You can also invest in security reserves, which are formed when a group of investors combine their funds so that an asset manager can purchase a large number of individual bonds.

There are four fundamental categories of bonds:

• Corporate. They are granted by institutions. Unlike shares, bonds issued by organizations do not confer ownership rights. They are less secure securities, but they typically compensate with higher rates of interest.

• Government bonds. Given by the government agency. It is a method for legislators to raise money without raising taxes. They can be an excellent option for the portfolio's generally secure portion.

- Municipal securities. Presented by cities, states, and counties.

- Agency obligations. Presented by government-affiliated institutions

The market interest rate determines the day-to-day value of an obligation. When selecting bonds, maturity and duration should be considered. Bonds with extended maturities will be significantly more affected by changes in average loan costs. Due to fluctuations in loan costs, securities with extended maturities are subject to a greater degree of risk; consequently, they offer higher yields (respects) and are therefore more attractive to investors.

- Premium. A few organizations assign a FICO score to each security in order to evaluate its quality. The yield decreases as the borrower's FICO score increases.

You can lose money on a security if you sell it before the maturity date for less than what you paid for it, or if the guarantor defaults on payments.

Typically, the duration over which you receive revenue payments from securities is two years.

Due to the fact that they do not all pay at the same time, investing in multiple securities can result in more regular payments.

It is possible to construct a security portfolio yielding monthly income. This can be obtained by purchasing various securities (typically six) that pay a premium on other dates.

Bonds are less susceptible to monetary loss than equities. Therefore, acquiring a few securities and a few equities can reduce portfolio losses. Bonds can be obtained from a number of sources, including investment and commercial institutions, brokers, and corporations.

The minimum investment required to purchase a single security is approximately $1,000, but securities are typically sold in increments of $5,000.

Developing My Company And My Life

In addition, I was not managing the highest degree of certainty falling off a six-month pity party. I didn't even know where to begin. Teresa and I were licensed Realtors, and I saw an advertisement in a magazine stating that a man named Craig Proctor would be teaching specialists how he sells so many properties.

My mother provided us with funds, and we went to his class. Using my mother's Mastercard, we decided to enlist him as a mentor for a course, and we were making haste. This meeting occurred in April 2009, and our first closings occurred in June 2009.

In 2009, Teresa and I established a land outreach group that was awarded the public Rookie of the Year grant. In 2010, Teresa and I won a public Quantum Leap grant, and our fortunes began to improve. In 2011, we won another Quantum Leap grant and were named Utah's Large Sales Team of the Year.

Another significant event transpired for us in 2011. Teresa and I had struggled with infertility for quite some time, but we desperately desired to start a family.

If you or someone you know has ever struggled with infertility, you know that it is an extremely emotional and distressing condition to endure. It is also extremely expensive. Teresa and I tried numerous systems and wealth remedies without success. As a result of additional tests, it was not set in stone that our primary option was in vitro fertilization with an extra advance known as ICSI. This was a truly novel technique that had only been around for two or three years; it had only a 20 percent chance of success and cost about $100,000.

I am embarrassed to admit that this was not an easy decision for me. We had only recently rebuilt our investment funds, so having children was probably not a realistic option. Fortunately, I am married to a woman who is not set in stone, and Teresa never considered it. She was persuaded that we should use our investment capital to test out this new method.

On May 16, 2011, we were privileged to meet Wyatt and Grace, two healthy children. I know that, like many other parents, having children drastically altered my life and outlook on everything. The egocentric, carefree person I was before they entered my life seems like a distant memory.

I began asking myself various questions. I considered what my motivation was. What drove me forward. What legacy I needed to leave behind. This multitude of thoughts began to enter my mind.

We were well served by the land sale. We had encountered some remarkable individuals. We had encountered and traveled to some incredible locations. We had accumulated substantial earnings. But I never felt a strong emotional connection to it. It was missing something.

I once heard Tony Robbins say, "Achievement without satisfaction is the ultimate letdown." I was unable to remove this notion from my mind. I was generating money as a Realtor and achieving success, but I lacked a sense of fulfillment. As another father, I've begun to consider my family's long-term financial future.

Prior to that point, I spent every dollar I earned, generally because I believed there was more where that came from. Nonetheless, living was no longer centered around work. It was essential for me to provide financially for my expanding family, as well as provide opportunities for us to share in memorable experiences and spend quality time together. I appreciate material possessions as much as the next person, but Teresa and I have always preferred experiences and excursions over material gifts for birthdays and Christmas, and we love to look back on our photos and reminisce about the wonderful occasions and beautiful places we have had the opportunity to visit. We have a townhouse in Hawaii (not my finest financial investment, coincidentally), and we travel there annually during the week surrounding Wyatt and Grace's birthdays. During one of these excursions, Wyatt inquired, "Father, how about you sell houses in Hawaii?"

It was a simple question, but it prompted me to contemplate where and what types of properties inspire me. I have traded a large number of properties over the years. From mobile residences to a few million-dollar properties. I have also invested in various types of real estate, ranging from discount deals and fix-and-flip properties to land enhancement deals and new construction homes.

In 2006, we purchased a vacation property in a mountain lake community. We were able to retain this home despite the upheaval of losing everything and renovating because the costs were covered by renters. It also provided a welcome respite from all the tension.

As I sat on the beach in Hawaii, I didn't have to ponder Wyatt's question for very long. I knew exactly what type of land inspires me. I adore country estates due to the fact that they are ordinarily situated in the most breathtaking locales on the planet, and they provide opportunities for unforgettable experiences with loved ones. I have also always enjoyed investment properties, particularly those with passive income.

At this point, I decided to incorporate my new requirements into my daily life and began to concentrate on acquiring Lifestyle Assets for our own speculation portfolio.

Lifestyle Assets combine the most intelligent solution imaginable. I became obsessed with this new automobile.

I altered my entire marketing strategy and objectives in order to assist others in comprehending and determining whether Lifestyle Assets are a suitable addition to a portfolio. I established a comprehensive platform to assist individuals in acquiring the most suitable Lifestyle Assets for their particular circumstances.

Understanding of Alternatives

How do you employ your skills to make money on the stock market? is the crucial question. You must recognize patterns and arrangements as they manifest. Following this is a potential application method. Norms are formulated. The patterns and locations where the rules for determining entry and exit points should be implemented are displayed on charts.

Based on the last increase or break, determine whether the congestion is a re-accumulation or a re-distribution. Until the congestion pattern indicates otherwise, assume this.

The Halt

We propose two steps: an average spread below the most recent reaction low, or the entry bar's spread below the entry bar. As soon as we have movement freedom, the stop will be reinforced. If the price does not respond within three bars, close the position. Then, do not wait for the halt to be activated.

Trade or Not?

If you do not invest in the market, you do not expose your money to risk. This trading strategy restricts exposure to between 10 and 15 percent of the total observation period. Approximately 85 to 90 percent of the time, you are not in the market. During an accumulation or distribution phase, it is possible to hold a position. Although there is nothing inherently wrong with this strategy, significant portions of the profits are at risk. The pattern could be one of distribution as opposed to accumulation. You must examine numerous charts before concluding that this strategy is viable and compatible with your trading style. This strategy requires considerable judgment. As a means of minimizing uncertainty, they should attempt to automate as many rules as feasible.

Trade Valuable Assets

Active trading is best suited for equities and/or futures that are in a phase of movement or trend, as opposed to securities that are in a state of constant sideways movement. The definition of a fluctuating value is highly subjective. Investor's Business Daily is among the top sources that provide lists of securities that outperform and outperform others.

Transferable securities may exhibit the following characteristics:

increased uncertainty

Having reached a new four-week peak

Investments in the rising era

Significantly upward or downward sloping 20-day moving average over the past month

The predominant prices in a particular market segment

Concise Summary

Remember that the objective of this game is to succeed, not to be in 90% of price moves. Open positions when specific patterns occur, and take profits when the target price is reached or at the first indication that supply exceeds demand.

These fundamental principles apply to all time horizons, such as day trading. Utilize weekly charts if your focus is long-term. This will result in numerous false alarms, but there are in fact limits. You can only make money by analyzing countless charts and drawing your entry points, exit points, and stop loss levels. Thus, you internalize these methods and make them appropriate. After that, you could achieve trading success. One of the most difficult aspects of trading is closing a position at the conclusion of an outbreak or during a purchasing surge. Simply convince yourself that you are a good person: everyone desires the stock, but you give yours away.

The General Motors study may serve as an example of how to design a trade system based on supply and demand. Create two schematics, one detailing what you should have done and the other detailing what you actually did. Learn through comparison. Recognize the forces at play during pivotal moments.

Application of the Elliott Wave Theory to the Real World

The Elliott Wave Theory is baffling to numerous speculators. We do not wish to discuss the ambiguity of this theory, but we will apply it to a trading strategy that should prove fruitful. This theory is among the finest Cycle theories because it allows for non-harmonious movements.

There are numerous approaches to trading securities. These approaches can be broadly classified as either fundamental or technical. Some specialists prefer to combine the two approaches for the most effective market strategy. The fundamental access includes bushels, hectares, consumption units, revenues, book values, and so on. Technical analysis examines past price movements and predicts future ones. Elliott published a series of articles in

1939 describing the fundamentals of Elliott waves. The Elliott Wave Theory is one of the most effective technical methods for market analysis, and anyone with a serious interest must incorporate it into their studies.

Is it possible to forecast pricing trends using Elliott Wave Theory and profit from this information? The answer is a qualified yes if the theory is not treated as an exact science. The Elliott Wave Theory permits both harmonic and nonharmonic course deviations. The majority of cycle theories are founded on harmonic movement principles. As soon as discordant movements occur, difficulty ensues.

The following Elliott Wave Theory summary condenses the concepts into a manageable size.

Two of the five waves in ascending movements are corrections. Contraproductive are falling movements. The irregular waves move in the same direction as the primary current. Straight waves travel in opposition to the primary current. The second shaft corrects the first. Blade 5 corrects blade 4. There are occasionally nine or more waves. Elliott resolves this issue by naming these extension movements.

The height of shaft 4 is greater than that of shaft 1. Elliott provides precise length proportions, such as the shaft 4 being shorter than the waves 3 and 5. However, it has been discovered that this is not always the case.

The movements are subdivided into one-degree smaller pulses. What does "one degree smaller" indicate? This query is challenging to answer, which is one reason why applying the theory is so challenging. One suggestion is to search in the subsequent lesser timeframe. If you have a daily chart, check the 30-minute chart for the lesser grade. The daily chart is identical to the next lesser degree, which also requires five waves to complete the first higher-order wave.

Triangular Adjustments

After a thrust, triangular corrections consist of a five-point pattern (ABCDE). The nature and position of such a pattern frequently permit inferences as to whether a reversal is imminent or not.

A-Shaped Adjustments

Length and duration of the first correction wave or A-shaped thrust correction are of the uttermost importance for determining the total correction's future course and the likelihood of a turnaround.

Observe the application of the A-wave (the initial correction wave to rise) to determine the type of correction and the price's likely direction after the correction is complete. Then, four probable price movements are displayed. If the length of the A correction wave is the same, we can deduce the following:

25% - 35%: Indicates a single wave of correction.

35% to 50%: A three-wave correction.

50% to 75%: Represents a five-wave correction.

Over seventy-five percent: a probable trend reversal.

Forecasting the Corrections

This price development may result in a reversal. The forces of supply and demand are at work here. A reaction at a distance of 75% from the starting location is more definitive than one at a distance of 25%.

Comprehending Options Vocabulary

Due to logic, the duration of the option is a factor. Normally, it would cost more to control an asset for a prolonged duration, such as five years as opposed to one. Alternately, if you only need the asset controlled for one day, it would be less expensive.

This is because the greater the asset's level of control, the greater the likelihood that something can occur to influence its price. If the property was only under your control for one day, it is unlikely that a significant real estate transaction involving your property will be reported on that day.

www.ingramcontent.com/pod-product-compliance
Lightning Source LLC
Chambersburg PA
CBHW050028130526
44590CB00042B/2076